JONAH

SALVATION BELONGS TO THE LORD

Kelly Mott

Jonah: Salvation Belongs to the LORD by Kelly Mott
© 2017 by Kelly Mott. All rights reserved.

Author photo © 2016 by Sierra Allmand. All rights reserved.

Cover design © 2015 by Margaret Grauke. All rights reserved.

Typesetting by: John Gjertsen

Editing by: Abigail Gjertsen

Mott, Kelly, 1982 – Jonah: Salvation Belongs to the LORD

Library of Congress Control Number: TBA

ISBN: 978-1-943974-30-6

10 9 8 7 6 5 4 3 2 1

BS1605.5 The Bible O.T. Jonah—Other.

BS680.R36 Repentance

BS1605.6M53 Missions

First Edition

Contents

To My Readers

I remember it well: a bearded man in robes stuck on the flannel board next to a rotund, jovial-looking whale. Jonah. We're dangerously familiar with it. If you are like I was, you convince yourself that you know the story, but you only focus on the first half of it and can't remember the last time you've actually read the book all the way through.

I'm here to tell you that Jonah is far more than a fish tale. It is the story of a man, a servant of the Lord, called to go to his enemies.

Jonah, though he is a prophet, is far from perfect, and it is perhaps more his failures than his successes that resonate with the modern-day reader. We can't easily identify with Elijah calling down fire from heaven and defeating the prophets of Baal (I Kings 18). But we can readily and personally relate to Jonah, disobedient and discontent.

In his introduction to Jonah in *The Message*, Eugene Peterson writes:

> Instead of being held up as an ideal to admire, we find Jonah as a companion in our ineptness. Here is someone on our level. Even when Jonah does it right (like preaching, finally, in Nineveh) he does it wrong (by getting angry at God). But the whole time, God is working within and around Jonah's very ineptness and accomplishing his purposes in him. Most of us need a biblical friend or two like Jonah[1].

I initially wanted to title this study "*Jonah: The Prodigal, Poetic, Penitent, Pouting Prophet*" to represent the many facets of his character and story, but in the end I decided against it. After all, Jonah isn't the main character of this narrative—God is. God is always the main character. Every biblical book and story is ultimately about God, His character, His glory, and His grand narrative that arches over all of our micro-narratives. This reality is reflected in the major themes we will trace in Jonah, like dominant patterns in a beautiful tapestry: **God's sovereignty, true obedience and true repentance, and God's love for the nations contrasted with our own religious elitism and hypocrisy**.

How to Use this Study

This Bible study was written for use in an 11-week, large- or small-group setting with individual weekly homework assignments which start after the Introduction meeting. The weekly homework is broken down into three days of assignments which should each take about 20 minutes to complete. The Introduction and final weeks have prompts for large group discussion, and the final week also includes an optional closing activity to help you remember the special insights God has shown you from Jonah!

My goal is to write questions that will make you slow down and think. Often there is not one specific answer to a question, so don't get bogged down if you are not sure. Just pray for the Holy Spirit to guide you into truth, write what you think the Bible is showing you, and be ready to discuss others' insights when you meet with your group. Also, if you get really stuck and there is a footnote superscript on that question, check the end of the week's material to see some excellent insights from commentators and theologians (as well as a few from myself!) If you are facilitating a discussion group, make sure you have read through the footnotes after you finish your own homework. They just might save you a few rabbit trails!

We often read faster when we're familiar with the ending, which can cause us to miss the intricacies of the story and the beauty of the narrative. Since scripture is God-breathed (2 Tim. 3:16), every detail in the Bible is included for a reason, and together we will examine word choices, repeated motifs, and perplexing non-endings. Perhaps the most important part of this Bible study is the last question of each week where space is provided for journaling as well as a "prayer prompt." Take advantage of this opportunity to spend time in worshipful reflection. You'll be glad you did.

Most of all, I want us to know God better as a result of this endeavor. That's the point. It doesn't matter if you can diagram a clever and intricate chiasm (a preview of things to come!) if you don't know the God about whom the chiasm is penned. Jonah is a purposefully structured and intricately woven book—and that is beautiful. But even more beautiful than that is the mercy and love of the God-of-second-chances which permeates the book.

Aren't you excited to get started now? I am thrilled to take this journey with you as we learn about Jonah, but even more about God. May praises be raised to the God of the universe to whom salvation belongs ultimately and eternally. Amen.

Kelly

---

[1] Peterson, Eugene. *The Message* (Colorado Springs: NavPress, 2002), 1664.

A note to the leaders

You have the privilege of engaging in ten weeks of study with your fellow participants. Your job is important—to pray for participants during the week, facilitate discussion, pull out answers, and, at times, be okay with silence. God is working in peoples' hearts during times of silence. You do not have to fill it, and you do not have to know all the answers! Pray for good discussion and for the Lord to be honored in your times of private study and group discussion times.

Please encourage everyone to complete their homework. Discussion will be far fuller and deeper when each member has already delved into Scripture on his/her own during the week! Consider encouragement and simple rewards for homework accountability. Model good study skills and accountability by completing your homework every week as well.

Facilitation is an important task—gently drawing out reserved participants, squelching unhelpful rabbit trails, and keeping the focus on God and His grand story through Jonah. May you be blessed and bless others over the next ten weeks. At the end of the book are some helpful hints to guide you in structuring your small groups and group time. Thank you for your role in this study!

See the Leaders' Guide at the end of the study for information about materials needed, discussion guidelines, and suggested timeframes for your time together.

Intro Week: Overview

Questions for Small Groups:

1. Briefly describe the God you see revealed in Jonah.

2. What surprised or stuck out to you? What questions do you have now that you have read it?

3. Did anything make you laugh? Is this book supposed to be (allowed to be?) funny, or not?

4. Based on your initial readings, what do you think the statement "Salvation belongs to the LORD" (2:9) means?

Three Major Themes in Jonah

What are the main topics or issues dealt with in Jonah? There are many recurring motifs and ideas in Jonah, but we will focus on these three major themes. We will represent each one with an easy-to-remember icon or symbol. These themes and their icons will be referenced throughout the rest of this study.

The first theme is **God's Sovereignty** (crown symbol). This means that God is all knowing, all powerful, and in control. Or, as theologian Abraham Kuyper said, "There is not a square inch in the entire creation about which Christ does not cry out, 'This is mine! This belongs to me!'"[1] God will prove Himself sovereign over Jonah's journey and ours as well.

Secondly, the book of Jonah exhibits the importance of **obedience and repentance from the heart** (heart symbol). We are often disobedient, and at other times obey out of fear or reluctantly, but the best results and blessings are found when obedience and repentance are true, free, and heartfelt.

Last, Jonah exhibits **God's love for the nations** (globe symbol). This is contrasted against religious elitism, hypocrisy, and entitlement: the feeling that we are more deserving of God's attention and blessings than others.

These three themes will be referenced throughout this study and will be woven together to create a strong reminder of the purpose of this powerful little book. **In your homework each week, a few questions will have an empty box below them. Decide which of the three theme(s) each question relates to most and draw the theme's symbol in the box.** This will help us trace our themes and pull them all together at the end of the study!

Signposts for the Journey into Jonah

There are three days of homework each week which should take about 20 minutes each (one hour a week total). In future weeks you should return to your group ready to discuss the week's homework, but if you fall behind on the homework, come to your group anyway! You will glean a lot from the discussion time. There are a few helpful footnotes at the end of each week with insights from commentators that should help you if you get stuck or confused. Turn to week one's homework to get an idea of what awaits you!

DAY 1

Week 1: Structure and Genre

I am excited that you are willing to journey together as we dive into the book of Jonah. I must warn you, the questions won't always be easy and the applications will make you think. If you've participated in a Bible study before, you know that many factors may make it difficult to complete this study. Sometimes it seems as though as soon as you commit to a study, life's obligations fight back, making it a challenge to find time to complete the homework and attend the meetings.

But don't think this pattern is a coincidence. I Peter 5:8 tells us that "your enemy the devil prowls around like a roaring lion looking for someone to devour." The last thing Satan wants is for one of God's children to get serious about studying God's Word. Satan may try to throw everything in the book at us as we undertake this study. Let's take up the full armor of God, defeat Satan's attacks, know the value of studying the Word, and run this race together with our eyes fixed on Jesus. I don't promise that it will be easy, but I do promise that studying God's Word and His character are always worth every effort. Are you ready, friend? Let's go!

Write a prayer to the Lord discussing your hopes in this study. What would you like to learn? What are your expectations? What are your fears and challenges? How would you like to be able to describe your relationship with Him at the end of this study?

Now, let's get to work! Today we are going to look at two big questions about the book of Jonah: What makes it a great story, and is it too good to be true?

Structure

You've probably already noticed repeated words, phrases, and ideas in the book of Jonah. The author uses these and other literary devices to guide the reader to the important messages in the book; the message is emphasized by the way it is presented. To see what the author is showing us and to unlock the meaning of Jonah for our lives, we have to work out these literary clues. Let's see what you can do!

1. Reread your ESV copy of Jonah. Try to ignore the chapter and verse divisions, which were added long after Jonah was written. The book divides neatly into two halves. Where do you think the break occurs?

2. Make up a title for each of the halves.

3. One element that occurs in both halves of the book is God telling Jonah to go to Ninevah. Find two more repeated elements.

    i.

    ii.

One of the most distinctive literary characteristics in Jonah is called *chiasm*, from the Greek letter X (*chi*). Ancient writers often used chiasms. "In a chiastic pattern, the elements in the second half of the structure invert the elements of the first half. The pattern may be long or short, very complex or very simple."[1] Another way to describe it is inverted parallelism. One simple example is the famous words of John F. Kennedy:

"Ask not what your country can do for you

but what you can do for your country."

with the X (*chi*) connecting the matching parts. Another way of writing it could be

A. (Ask not what) your country
  B. can do for you
  B'. (but what) you can do for
A'. your country

Chiasms can come in different forms, such as:

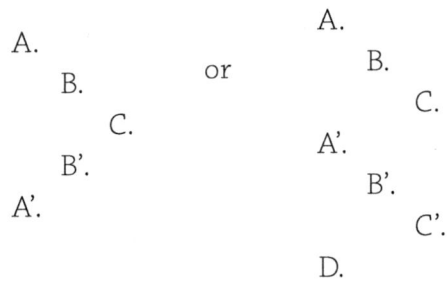

```
A.                      A.
    B.          or          B.
        C.                      C.
    B'.                     A'.
A'.                             B'.
                                    C'.
                        D.
```

Although chiasms can be fun to discover, they are pointless unless they reveal or reinforce meaning. Their stepped structure is meant to help us focus on the main point of the passage (think "X marks the spot"). The focal points of a chiasm can be found in any or all of the following:

- the reflected beginning and end (bookends)

- the climactic center

- the unique element that deviates from the expected pattern (D in the last example). This is like a song that ends with an unexpected note.

Think about how patterns can set us up for certain expectations. In the nursery story, "The Three Little Pigs," the first pig builds his house of straw. The wolf knocks, the pig won't let him in ("not by the hair of my chinny-chin-chin"), and then the wolf huffs and puffs and blows the house in. Similar events unfold with the second pig, who built his house of sticks. The third pig, however, builds his house of bricks, and after the same chinny-chin-chin/huff puff exchange, it proves too strong for the wolf to blow down.

Now let's examine this simple storytelling strategy as a literary element. The storyteller sets up a repetetive pattern that the listener expects to continue, so when the pattern is broken, the listener should ask himself, "why is this outcome different?" This is like an unresolved, unbalanced section of a chiasm that does not have a match anywhere else in the structure. A deviation from the previous pattern should lead us to the main message of the work.

4. With these points in mind, what message(s) is the storyteller trying to emphasize in "The Three Little Pigs"? (*Hint:* what is the moral of the story?)

See, you learned something new today! Chiasms take some practice, but I've found that they are well worth the effort! Now it's time to try your hand at chiasm in Jonah.

5. You already know where Jonah breaks in half. Try to outline its main sections into a chiasm. I'll give you the outline letters and get you started with the first three sections.

    A. *Jonah's commissioning and flight (1:1-3)*
    　　B. *Jonah and the pagan sailors (1:4-16)*
    　　　　C. *Jonah's grateful prayer (1:17-2:10)*

    A'.

    　　B'.

    　　　　C'.

    D.

6. Based on the structure of your chiasm, what is the message of the book of Jonah?[2]

7. Before discovering the chiastic structure, would you have pointed to this as the main point of the book? How does it change your view of the book and its themes? Explain. (Remember, the box below reminds you to draw in the icon of the theme(s) from page 11 that matches this question.)

DAY 2

Genre

8. How does the book of Jonah seem different from other books of prophecy (e.g. Daniel, Isaiah, Hosea)?[3]

Did the events in Jonah really happen? Is Jonah a historical, factual account or a moral tale meant to teach, like a parable? This is not a question about the Bible's inerrancy or inherent trustworthiness. Certain books frequently use figures of speech and poetic devices to describe ideas rather than narrate the details of history (e.g. Song of Solomon, Proverbs, Psalms, Ecclesiastes, the parables, parts of Revelation). The question is, do we read Jonah as a factual historical account or a parable that was fashioned for narrative effect?

9. Consider the biblical passages and elements of Jonah on the facing page. Write an "H" next to each one that supports the interpretation of Jonah as a historical account, and an "P" next to ones that support its categorization as a parable. Then write a brief explanation of why you think the item supports that interpretation. *(Some of these can be either or both, depending on your explanation.)*

10. Now that you've filled out the chart, what do you think? Is Jonah historically accurate, a literary lesson, or a combination? Explain (before you go peek at the note at the end).[4]

DAY 3

11. Let's look at one more piece of evidence. How did Jesus treat the book of Jonah? Read Matthew 12:38-41 and Luke 11:29-32. What is the sign of Jonah?

12. How does the sign of Jonah relate to Jesus?

H/P?	Passage or Story Element	Why?
P	2 Samuel 12:1-7	*Nathan's story was specifically cooked up to show David his sin. It wasn't an historical event.*
	2 Kings 14:23-25	
	Joel 1:1, Micah 1:1, Haggai 1:1, etc.	
	The location of Jonah in the Bible (look at the books before and after it)	
	The ending	
	The unusual "hero"	
	The crazy big fish!	
	The funny, ironic tone	
	The literary structure (e.g. repetition, chiasm)	
	The magic beanstalk??	
	The result of Jonah's preaching	
	The large number of questions	
	Other:	

13. Does Jesus' use of Jonah support its historical accuracy, its symbolic message, or both? Explain.[5]

14. Why did the author include elements like patterns, irony, and moral instruction (e.g. the contrasts drawn between Jonah and God) rather than write a factual "newspaper report" of the events?[6]

15. How does its grounding in history make us read Jonah differently than a children's story or fairy tale?

16. Why do you think God went to the trouble to engineer the crazy train of events described in Jonah and equip an author to polish them into a gem of ironic narrative? Why do you think He wants you to study this unusual book at this point in your life?

---

[1] Bryan D. Estelle, *Salvation Through Judgment and Mercy: The Gospel According to Jonah* (Phillipsburg, NJ: P&R, 2005), 49.

[2] Chiasm helps us determine both the structure and the crux of the passage.
    A. Jonah's commissioning and flight (1:1-3)
       B. Jonah and the pagan sailors (1:4-16)
          C. Jonah's grateful prayer (1:17-2:10)
    A'. Jonah's recommissioning and compliance (3:1-3a)
       B'. Jonah and the pagan Ninevites (3:3b-10)
          C'. Jonah's angry prayer (4:1-4)
    D. Jonah's lesson about compassion (4:5-11)
Mark Futato, *Jonah. Study Notes in the ESV Study Bible* (Wheaton, IL: Crossway Bibles, 2008), 1686.

[3] "The book is given over almost exclusively to a narrative about the life of the prophet, rather than concentrating on the message from the Lord through his prophet. In this regard, Jonah resembles more the narratives about the prophets in the historical books of the Bible than the books that consist mainly of prophetic utterances." O. Palmer Robertson, *The Christ of the Prophets, Abridged Edition* (Phillipsburg, NJ: P&R, 2008), 157.

[4] "It is impossible to be dogmatic either way. There are plausible, but not provable arguments to counter the points against a historical reading." Tremper Longman III and Raymond B. Dillard, *An Introduction to the Old Testament, 2nd ed.* (Grand Rapids: Zondervan, 2006), 445.

[5] "When Jesus uses the account of Jonah as the principal model for his own three-day death and resurrection experience, the reality of Jonah's experience is clearly removed from the realm of non historical irrelevance... If Jonah's three-day descent into Sheol is to be regarded as historical fiction, then the parallel with the experience of Jesus inevitably would open the door to regarding his three-day burial and subsequent resurrection as also fictional in character...Instead of being viewed as a didactic story, the book should be characterized as didactic history." Robertson, 158-60.

[6] "With its unexpected twists and turns the plot successfully retains our attention throughout. Superfluous details are omitted, and the text abounds in word-plays and other compositional techniques. Everything indicates that is has been composed by an author who has used his literary skills to the full." T. Desmond Alexander, *Jonah: An Introduction and Commentary* (Downers Grove, IL: IV Press, 1988), 51.

DAY 1

Week 2: The Prodigal Prophet

Jonah 1:1-3

Sometimes we feel distant from the stories in the Bible. Strange names of both people and places sometimes isolate their "then" from our "now." After all, they lived so long ago and in such different cultures, how could we possibly relate? But that is the beauty of Scripture—it is eternally relate-able.

The book of Jonah is no different. At its core, the book of Jonah is about a man called to go to his enemies in love. Perhaps that thought brings this story a little closer to home. It is not just about a distant land and a long-deceased prophet—it is about obedience to God's difficult-to-follow commands. How would you respond if God gave you such an audacious assignment? Would you run away? Would you go, but grumble constantly? Would you truly love your enemies and obey God's assignment with joy?

If you've been relying on the printout of Jonah from the ESV, it's time to find Jonah in your own Bible! After the books written in part by David (the Psalms) and Solomon (Proverbs, Ecclesiastes, and Song of Solomon) come the Major (i.e. longer) Prophets: Isaiah, Jeremiah (plus Lamentations since it was written by Jeremiah), Ezekiel, and Daniel. Once you get past them you are getting warm.

The Minor Prophets are the last twelve books of the Old Testament, and they used to be all written on the same scroll. Jonah is tucked in as the fifth book of the twelve Minor Prophets. Jonah is in a grouping with the first six minor prophets, which date from the period of Assyrian power. Within that group the books are not necessarily chronological,[1] but their first letters do spell out the word "HJAOJM." Hope that helps! ;)

"Propheteering"

1. Read Jonah 1:1-3. Last week we looked up the first verses of Joel, Micah, and Haggai. Zechariah and Malachi begin the same way. What do these verses tell us about the calling or role of a prophet?

2. Read Jeremiah 1:4-19. What can you learn from this example about the role of an Old Testament prophet?

3. Read I Corinthians 14:1-4. What are the purposes of prophecy according to this New Testament passage?

4. Are there current-day prophets? Why or why not? How does God speak now?[2]

History

After the time of Solomon, the nation of Israel was divided into two kingdoms, the North (called Israel, because it contained most of the original twelve tribes) and the South (called Judah, for its dominant tribe). For years they coexisted as separate sovereign nations that made treaties and went to war mostly independently of one another. God assigned prophets to both kingdoms, and both kingdoms were eventually toppled under His judgment.

Jonah was a prophet during the Divided Kingdom, which is an unfamiliar time period to a lot of us. To help get yourself oriented to his place in history, examine the timeline of selected events, kings, and prophets below.[3] Remember, these B.C. dates are ascending right to left because this is all before the advent of Christ.

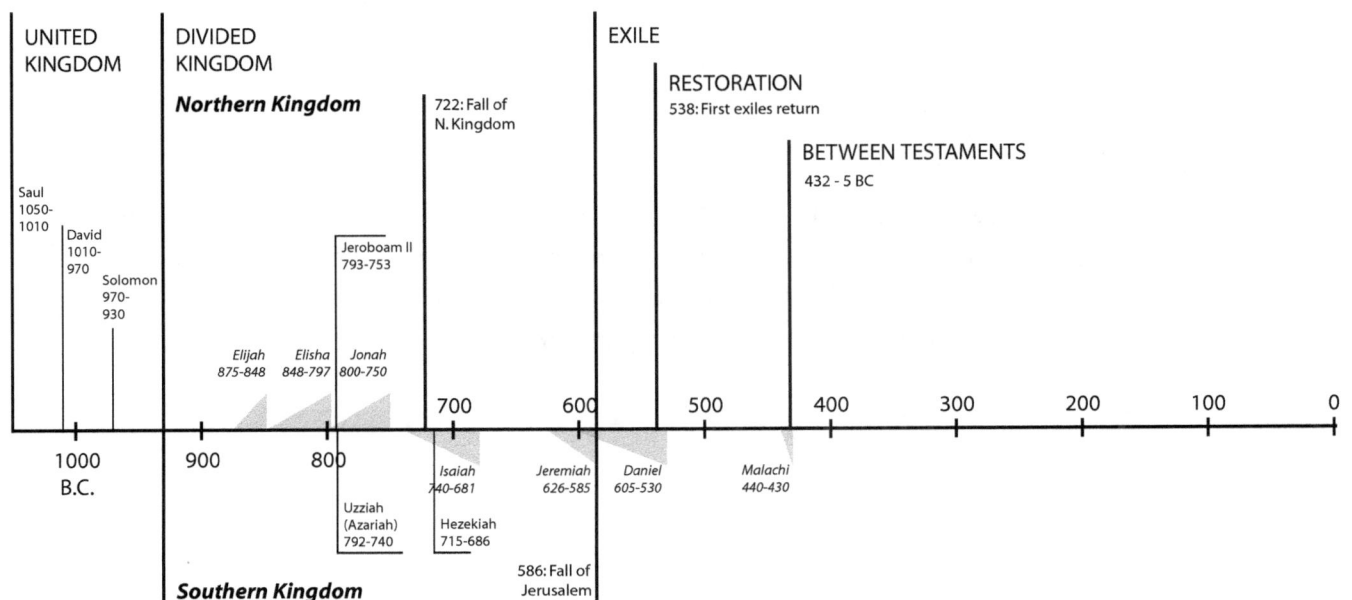

5. Circle or highlight these familiar folks on the timeline: King David, King Solomon, Elijah the prophet, and Daniel the prophet. (Remember, the dates listed for some of these people are just scholarly guesses.) Add our favorite Prophet, Priest, and King: Jesus (born pretty close to 1 A.D.).

6. Revisit II Kings 14:23-25. Which kingdom is Jonah from? Who was king there during Jonah's ministry? Circle or highlight Jonah and the king he served on the timeline.

DAY 2

7. Read Genesis 10:11-12. What region contains Nineveh? How is Nineveh described both here and in Jonah 1:1-2?

8. In Jonah's time, Assyria was a threatening military force, but for his later readers, it was even more terrifying. Read God's words to Isaiah (after Jonah's time) in Isaiah 8:4 and to all Israel (also called Ephraim) in Hosea 9:1-3 and 11:1-5. What is going to happen to Israel, why, and by what means?

9. Read the fulfillment of these prophecies in 2 Kings 17:1-8. Go back and circle or highlight the Fall of the Northern Kingdom on your timeline. What kind of relationship did Nineveh and Assyria have to Israel, the Northern Kingdom? How does this information affect our reading of the book of Jonah?

10. What specifically about Nineveh grieved the Lord? Flip two books past Jonah to Nahum, read Nahum 1:1 for context, and make a list of grievances from the following passages.

   Nahum 1:11:

   Nahum 3:1:

   Nahum 3:16:

   Nahum 3:18:

   Nahum 3:19:

11. In Jonah's day, Assyria was a major enemy of Israel, but he would not have known that they would be the instrument of God's judgment of the Northern Kingdom. With this distinction in mind, why do you think Jonah was reluctant to go to Nineveh?[4]

12. How would you feel if you knew that it were probable that the wicked Nation X would annihilate your beloved country less than a century from now? Now imagine that God has called you to go preach to Nation X so that it might repent and He could have mercy upon it in spite of all its evil deeds. How would you react?[5]

13. Do you have any enemies? Before you say "no," think a minute. You probably have enemies that are long-term, even lifelong. For instance, consider a neighbor or co-worker who consistently works for your harm, an abusive family member, those hostile to your country, or enemies of the church. List the long-term enemies you have here (use initials for privacy).

DAY 3

14. Would you consider temporary or minor "opponents" your enemies? For example, a temporary enemy might be a friend or a child during a fight, a spouse during a tense time in your marriage, a co-worker who undermines you, a church member(!) who gossips about you, or a neighbor who irritates you? Explain.

15. What is the difference between how you handle these two groups of "enemies"?

16. Has God called you to go to any of your enemies?

17. Israel and Judah—both kingdoms of Israel—are sovereignly judged and dismantled or exiled due to disobedience. God uses Assyria and later Babylon as tools to do this. How does this affect your view of history? of your country's future? of our "enemies"?

18. Review Jonah 1:1-3 one more time. What do you learn about God in these first verses?

19. Read Matt. 5:43-48 and write a prayer asking for God's strength and
    compassion to help you love your enemies.

[1] Kenneth L. Barker, ed., "Introduction to the Book of the Twelve, or the Minor Prophets," *The NIV Study Bible* (Grand Rapids: Zondervan, 2002) 1341.

[2] There are two major schools of thought on this topic: cessation (from the word cease) and continuation. "Cessationists usually believe the miraculous gifts [such as tongues, prophecy and healing] were given only for the foundation of the Church, during the time between the coming of the Holy Spirit on Pentecost, c. AD 33 (see Acts 2) and the fulfillment of God's purposes in history, usually identified as either the completion of the last book of the New Testament or the death of the last Apostle." "Cessationists View," *Monergism.com*, CPR Foundation, http://www.monergism.com/directory/link_category/Spiritual-Gifts/Cessationists-View-Articles/. Advocates of the continuation of charismatic gifts believe such gifts are still given and used for the church today.

[3] Timeline dates from Barker, *NIV Study Bible*.

[4] "Nineveh was the most powerful city in the world, the seat of the Assyrian Empire whose military threatened to overrun Israel and its neighbors. Doing anything that in any way benefited Assyria would have been seen as suicidal for Israel." Timothy Keller, *Counterfeit Gods: The Empty Promises of Money, Sex, and Power, and Only Hope that Matters* (New York: Penguin, 2009), 134.

[5] The theme and questions about enemies and God's love for those outside the church were inspired by Eric Kapur, "The Book of Jonah" (Unpublished class notes, Orlando Grace Church, 2005).

DAY 1 — Week 3: The Prodigal Prophet's Plight: part 1

Jonah 1:3-9

We don't know much about Jonah before the book starts. From a scant few cross references we know that he was a Jewish prophet. We know his father's name. And we know that he served under King Jeroboam II. To try and fill in some of the gaps, I'm going to take us on an exercise I like to refer to as "sanctified imagination."

Jonah loved to hear the words of the Lord. After all, he was a well-known prophet and likely earned this reputation by obediently speaking the words of the Lord. He also loved his people and was waiting along with his fellow Israelites for the coming of the Messiah. He worshipped, kept the law, and served his God. He was faithful, religious, and patriotic...until one day God asked him to do the unthinkable.

I can't back up these "sanctified imaginings" with chapter and verse, but I hope they help us imagine where Jonah was coming from. Let's remember that the goal of this study is not to put Jonah on trial, but to understand the great mercy of Jonah's God. With this in mind, let's get our feet wet!

Going AWOL

1. Jonah's biography is almost a blank, but we have his name, and names in the Bible are usually significant! Jonah means "dove." Read Hosea 7:11. What qualities are associated with doves in the Bible? How could this apply to Jonah?

2. "Son of Amittai" (1:1) means "son of my faithfulness." How might this name apply to Jonah?

3. Read Jonah 1:1-10. What was Jonah's specific assignment? Why?

4. Where did Jonah go instead?[1] Why?

5. Read Psalm 139:1-18. What does this psalm have to say about fleeing from God's presence?

6. It's time to grab some colored pencils or pens and mark up your Bible or the ESV copy you printed the first week. For Jonah chapter 1:

   • Draw an "up" arrow over every occurrence of "up" words and phrases (like arise, go up, etc.) in these verses. Note: Some translations will make the repetition of these Hebrew words more obvious than others. If your version is unclear, try the ESV or NASB at www.biblegateway.com.

   • Draw a "down" arrow over every occurrence of "down" words and phrases.

   • Now circle every occurrence of the word "but."

   What pattern do you see? What do you think it means?[2]

7. What phrase occurs at the beginning and end of verse 3? Why is this repeated?

8. What is your initial impression of Jonah, the man? What are his emotions at the end of chapter 1? What are his rationalizations like? Can you identify with him? Explain.

DAY 2

9. What is/are your current assignment(s), as you understand them? How faithful and obedient are you to your current assignments?

Weather Alert

10. What powerful and descriptive words are used to illustrate the storm?[3] Who is responsible for the storm (and all storms)?

11. What actions did the sailors take when threatened by the storm? What do we learn about the sailors' backgrounds based on their actions?

12. What was Jonah doing during this life-threatening storm? Why is this significant?[4,5]

13. What does the Captain say to Jonah? Who does this sound like from earlier in the book? What is the point?[6,7]

14. How did the sailors determine who to blame for the storm? According to Proverbs 16:33, is this a legitimate way to make decisions? What does this show about our God?

☐

15. In the left column of the chart below, write the questions the sailors pose to Jonah in 1:8-9. Across from them, write Jonah's answers to each of the questions. *Hint*: there will be unmatched entries in both columns.

DAY 3

Sailors' questions to Jonah	Jonah's answers

16. Now find the unmatched "blanks" in your columns. Which answers does Jonah omit? Why? What information does he supply unasked?

17. What seems ironic about Jonah's answers to the sailors' questions?[8]

18. What do we call a person who says one thing while living like the opposite is true? Before we get all condescending, let's be honest. Are you like Jonah? Are you quick to affirm God's sovereignty, but—in certain situations—struggling with unbelief and disobedience? Explain.

19. "No past privilege, nor all past privileges together; no past obedience, nor fruitfulness in service, can ever substitute for present obedience to the word of God."[9] Have you been content to accept a static relationship with God, avoiding His call to the next level of obedience (and reward)?

20. Write a prayer to the Maker of sea and dry land, praising Him for His creative control and sovereignty over everything and asking Him to help your unbelief (Mark 9:24).

---

[1] "While the location of Tarshish is much disputed, one thing is agreed upon by all: Tarshish is in exactly the opposite direction of Nineveh." Estelle, 36.

[2] "*Went down* is also a euphemism for death. The suggestion is that each step away from the presence of the Lord is one step closer to 'going down' to death." Futato, 1687.

[3] "The storm must have been ferocious because men experienced on the sea do not grow uneasy quickly at the first sight of foul weather." "Literally translated 'the ship expected itself to crack up.' Or as another author says (with tongue in cheek?), the ship is about to become 'a nervous wreck.'" Estelle, 41.

[4] "The storm that so alarmed the crew served only to rock Jonah into deeper slumber, blissfully unaware of all the trouble he is causing." Leslie C. Allen, *The Books of Joel, Obadiah, Jonah and Micah*, New International Commentary on the Old Testament (Downers Grove, IL: William B. Eerdmans, 1976), 207.

[5] "The Greek translation of the Old Testament, the Septuagint, suggests that the captain may only have found him because he was snoring! Certainly he was in a deep sleep, perhaps of sheer exhaustion, caused by the total dissipation of his energies in running from God; perhaps in relaxation, now that he felt the crisis was over." Sinclair B. Ferguson, *Man Overboard!: A Study of the Life of Jonah* (Wheaton, IL: Tyndale House, 1982), 37.

[6] "The words must have seemed to Jonah like a haunting echo from the past, exposing once more the guilt of his flight from God. Now God had sent this pagan to arouse him to his duties." Ferguson, 38.

[7] "The repetition of [the Hebrew words] parodies closely Jonah's initial summons from God. Each word mocks him." Alexander, 103.

[8] "The implication of the confession of faith is that the source of the storm is none other than Yahweh who made the sea. The wonder is that Jonah can recite such a creed and yet show disrespect to the commands of the God whose sovereignty it celebrates." Allen, 210.

[9] Ferguson, 20.

DAY 1

Week 4: The Prodigal Prophet's Plight: part 2

Jonah 1:10-16

Most of us know Romans 8:28, which reads, "And we know that for those who love God all things work together for good, for those who are called according to His purpose." But does that verse really mean all things? Can God work through our screw-ups?

I have a story for you which I'm more than a little embarrassed to share. As an assignment for one class in seminary, I was required to attend an Alcoholics Anonymous meeting and write a paper about community and inclusion. I dutifully went to the meeting and was greeted heartily by about 30 AA members. I took my seat and we began the meeting. The topic of the night was surrender and I was excited—though I am not addicted to alcohol, I struggle with other addictions and I can readily relate to the difficulty of surrender.

Each member was given the opportunity to share their thoughts about surrender after beginning their thoughts with the iconic, "Hello, my name is _____ and I'm an alcoholic." I listened to the other 29 people share wisdom, thoughts, and epiphanies about their struggles, and desire to surrender. As the talking continued I began to become nervous. My blood pressure rose. They were getting closer to me. I didn't know what to say. I didn't want to feel like an outsider—and I certainly didn't want these welcoming and brave people to think I was not touched by their stories just because I did not share their addiction.

So I lied.

When it was my turn, I said, "Hi, my name is Kelly and I'm an alcoholic." I had rationalized that the lie would be the right thing to do to support these people and feel a part of the group. However—as most lies do—mine grew exponentially and I kept making up more and more details about a fake story and a falsified struggle with alcoholism so as not to be exposed in my lie. And my guilt haunted me.

I hated how quickly it had gotten out of hand and how wrong my rationalizations were. I was sharing my woes with a co-worker a few weeks later and relating to her how much I regretted my decision and how I wish I could have done it over again. I told her that I had admitted my wrongness and then said, "I am so thankful that God is shows His grace to me when I mess up like I did in that AA meeting." To which my co-worker replied, "What's grace?" I then was able to explain a little about God's character and mercy to sinners in that moment. God had taken my screw-up and turned it in to something good: a platform for sharing the gospel. And for that I am thankful. We can be placed back on the path of obedience no matter how far we've strayed.

Hot Water

1. Think of a time when you knowingly disobeyed God. Try to remember the state of your heart at the time. Why did you do it? What was your motivation? How were you rationalizing the decision?

2. Re-read Jonah 1:1-16 and describe the situation where we left off from our study last week. What is Jonah's predicament?

3. What was Jonah's suggestion to calm the sea?

4. Do you interpret Jonah's proposal as a noble sacrifice, a foolish attempt to escape punishment and/or avoid his assignment, or something else? Explain your theory of his motivation.

5. How do the sailors respond to Jonah's proposal? What does this action tell you about the character of the sailors?

6. When their plans fail, the sailors pray. How is this prayer different than their previous petition in verse 5? What do they seem to understand about the Lord, based on this prayer?[1]

DAY 2

Man Overboard

7. The same Hebrew verb, which the ESV translates "hurled," is repeated twice in this passage. Circle them both (*Hint if you have a different translation:* v. 4,15). What connection should we make between the two?[2]

8. Jonah gets wet, and the sea gets calm. What three actions did the sailors do next? How do these actions complete the ironic contrast between Jonah and the sailors?

9. Look back over the chapter for three mentions of the sailors' fear. How has their fear changed at each point (*Hint:* v. 5, 10, and 16)?

10. What do the mariners call God in verse 6? What do they call Him in verse 14? Why is this change important?[3,4]

11. Jonah's elitist refusal to bring God's message to a pagan city was overruled by a sovereign God. What does this section reveal about God's character and purposes?

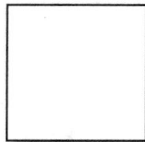

12. Read Mark 4:35-41. Name at least three similarities between the situations of Jesus and Jonah.

13. What is the difference between their motivations for sailing?

14. What are the "storms" in your life right now? What challenges do you have to deal with, whether you want to or not? What consequences are you facing from your past disobedience?

15. How do you make sense of the truth that God is responsible for all of life's storms?

16. How can a fresh attempt to reconcile life's pain with God's sovereignty and goodness influence your understanding of your current storms?

17. "[E]xtreme trouble, storm-trouble, strips us to the essentials and reveals the basic reality of our lives."[5] How has storm-trouble exposed the false supports you had grown dependent upon in fair weather? What true anchors emerged to take their place?

18. Read Isaiah 43:1-3a. Write a prayer to your Lord asking for true anchors and faith-filled obedience through the current storms in your life.

---

[1] "To avoid casting Jonah overboard the sailors make a valiant effort to bring the ship to shore. They struggle, however, in vain. Whereas they had previously cried to their gods, now they call to the Lord. Their reference to an innocent man does not imply that Jonah is guiltless; rather, the sailors are worried lest in casting Jonah into the sea, they themselves will be held accountable for his death. Like their captain, they too recognize the absolute sovereignty of God." Alexander, 106.

[2] "Interestingly, the sailors' action parallels closely the picture of God hurling a storm at the sea; their ability to hurl, however, cannot match that of the Lord." Alexander, 103.

[3] LORD in all capital letters indicates the use of the Hebrew word Yahweh, the covenant name of God given to Abram in Genesis 12 and used again in Exodus 20 with the giving of the Ten Commandments (among other references!). Lord (not in all caps) represents the word Elohim, a more general name for God as a sovereign higher power. Elohim is used in scripture in reference to both the Hebrew God and pagan deities or 'gods' in the general sense. Walter A. Elwell, "God, Names of," *Baker's Evangelical Dictionary of Biblical Theology* (1996): 1897, https://www.studylight.org/dictionaries/bed/g/god-names-of.html.

[4] "If Jonah has sunk in the hearers' estimation and the seamen have risen, the author has remained true to a basic tenet: Yahweh has emerged as the hero. The story begins with a moral rule and ends with his worship." Allen, 212.

[5] Eugene H. Peterson, *Under the Unpredictable Plant: An Exploration in Vocational Holiness* (Grand Rapids: William B. Eerdmans, 1992), 71.

Week 5: The Poetic (and Preserved!) Prophet

DAY 1

Jonah 1:17-2:10

The break-up that dashed the future you dreamt of for so long and thought would come to fruition. The pink slip that made you feel abandoned by the company to whom you were nothing but loyal. The phone call bearing terrible, irreversible news. The fight that made you think reconciliation would be impossible. The dreams, expectations, and hopes which fail to come true.

We've all experienced trials like these. We cannot avoid them, but we can determine how to face them. God does not waste our pain. He corrects our paths gently at some times and more forcefully at others, but He does not waste pain. First Peter 1:6-7 (NIV) says, "In all this you greatly rejoice, though now for a little while you may have had to suffer grief in all kinds of trials. These have come so that the proven genuineness of your faith—of greater worth than gold, which perishes even though refined by fire—may result in praise, glory and honor when Jesus Christ is revealed." I once read a poem that described God as a metalworker holding gold in a crucible over the fire. The temperature slowly rose and the gold began to bubble in the flames, releasing the impurities and dross hidden deep within its solid state. The heat rose and the dross was skimmed away; the gold looked cleaner, but the master refiner was not satisfied. The poem concluded by saying that God knew the refining process was complete when He could see Himself in the gold.[1]

What a picture of our lives! Trials are painful because they turn up the heat to remove impurities from deep within us like pride, sin, selfishness, love of the world, guilt, shame, and doubt. Our trials and sanctification will continue until all the dross is taken away and we are free to reflect Jesus, the Heavenly Refiner. We must recognize trials not as crazy coincidences, or meaningless tortures, or vengeful punishments, but as the outworking of God's plan from eternity past to purify His saints. Trials will come. The question is: are we going to trust Him to refine our faith in the midst of our pain?

Divine Appointment

1. Is the fish a central character in this book? Why does it get such a big role in most peoples' minds?

2. Last week we left the sailors making passionate vows and thankful sacrifices, but meanwhile something even more dramatic is happening beneath the ship. Read Jonah 1:17-2:10. Copy the last verse of chapter 1 out of your Bible below.

3. Name at least three purposes that the "great fish" and Jonah's experience in it accomplish.[2,3]

4. Do you find it hard to believe the fish's miraculous appearance and/or Jonah's preservation within it? Why or why not? Does this plot twist undercut the book's credibility, or has the reader been prepared for it? Explain.

Gutsy Prayer

5. What is the first (recorded) thing Jonah does after being swallowed by the fish? How is v. 2-9 formatted differently in your Bible than the preceding chapter? What does this change indicate?

6. If you were in Jonah's situation, what would you be praying? Why?[4]

For the rest of our time together, pull out the copy of Jonah that you received at the beginning of the study and some colored pens or pencils. Read the prayer of 2:2-9 closely and mark repeated words or ideas with matching colors or shapes.

7. What patterns or connections do you notice?

One storytelling style in Hebrew literature reads like a newscast: it summarizes the main action, then backs up and tells it again with more details. Think about the creation of humans in Genesis 1 on the sixth day, then the longer story of Adam and Eve being formed from the dust/rib in Genesis 2. This type of narration, called synopsis-resumption/expansion, is used in Jonah's prayer. Find the synopsis (or main summary) part and draw a box around it on your copy.

DAY 2

8. Verse 2 refers to Sheol, the Hebrew word for the realm of the dead. It's not the same idea as "hell"; the Greek equivalent is Hades. Read Job 17:16 and 38:17. What details about Sheol can you glean from these verses?

9. According to verse 3 in this psalm, who cast him into the deep? According to chapter one, who hurled Jonah overboard? How can we understand both declarations to be true?[5]

Find the transitional words that indicate a change in direction or thought (e.g. "yet," "but") and mark them with a new color.

-   Then go through, line by line, and in the margin write a (+) next to positive events or feelings and a (-) next to the negative events or feelings.

-   Draw a line where the major shift from negative to positive words occurs.[6]

Now take the line you drew at the turning point of the prayer. Reviewing the repeated words and ideas you marked, can you trace a chiasm (nested pairs of matching verses radiating from the center) within verses 4-8? Use big brackets in the margin to connect the pairings you see (ignore the verse numbering divisions in your analysis). (*Hint:* the pattern is A, B, C, C', B', A')

10. How does the deliberate structure of the chiasm dramatize the content of the prayer?

11. The second half of verse 4, "yet I shall again look upon your holy temple," stands out as a puzzling positive in a sea of negative descriptions. What is Jonah feeling here? Is he desperately optimistic, supremely confident that he will be saved, or determined to look to God in prayer? Now that you have the chiasm worked out, it should help you decide. What do the lines that match up with verse 4 have to say about God? What does this imply about Jonah's state of mind in verse 4?

12. Draw a box around the section of the prayer that contains Jonah's conclusion. What does he seem to learn (or re-affirm)?

13. What major "character" is perplexingly unmentioned in this prayer? Do you think Jonah's prayer is offered with or without knowledge of verse 10? Explain.

DAY 3

The Sign of Jonah

14. What does the fish do to Jonah in v. 10? Do you think that word choice is important? Why or why not?[7,8]

15. Most of the time Jonah was inside the fish, they were swimming back toward Nineveh. What does this reveal about the way God deals with His people?

16. Jonah has gone to the gates of Sheol and been brought back to life. What is God ultimately trying to teach Jonah about Himself through this near-death experience? Is he really changed?[9,10,11,12]

17. Read Mark 15:33-34. Name at least three ways that Jesus' experience of death is similar to Jonah's time in the belly of the fish.

18. Explain "Salvation belongs to the LORD!" in your own words. What are the implications for Israel, God's chosen people, and what are the implications for the (pagan) nations?

19. Jonah displayed a confident hope that God would listen and be merciful in spite of his own wilful disobedience, God's seeming abandonment, and the desperate situation he (justifiably) found himself in. Do you struggle to approach God boldly with a prayer for mercy for any similar reasons? Begin your prayer below by confessing your fears honestly, and then encourage your heart by recounting God's character as described in Jonah 2:8.

20. Continue writing your prayer using any aspects of Jonah's prayer that fit your situation. Whether you are desperate at the gates of Sheol, rejoicing in God's merciful provision, or recommitting your life with thankful vows, look upon His holy temple with hope!

1 "The Refiner's Fire," *The Friend: A Religious and Literary Journal*, 77, no. 45 (1904): 357, http://books.google. com/.

2 "The action is about to come to a full halt in order to leave Jonah alone with his God...Jonah on the brink of death is about to experience a profound encounter with the living God." Estelle, 75.

3 "The fish was not an instrument of God's judgment, but rather of his salvation, since it saved Jonah from death by drowning." Longman and Dillard, 447.

4 "Jonah in the belly of the fish was in the worst trouble imaginable. We naturally expect him to pray a lament. What we get, though, is its opposite, a psalm of praise, in the standard thanksgiving form." Peterson, *Under the Unpredictable Plant*, 102.

5 "In theological language Jonah is reflecting on the difference between secondary causes and primary causes." Ferguson, 54. Think of a game of billiards. The colored ball is hit by the cue ball which is hit by the cue stick, operated by the billiard player. In once sense we can say that the cue ball caused the colored ball to move-- in the terms above this would be the secondary or proximate cause because it is closest to observed result. However, from a different perspective we can see that the player controlling the cue stick is the true initiator of the movement. This bigger movement is termed the primary or ultimate cause. These distinctions are often beneficial when thinking about God's sovereignty and observed actions in the world.

6 "At length the downward journey ceases and Jonah's descent is dramatically reversed. This change in the direction of Jonah's movement brings to and end a series of descending steps which may be traced back to the beginning of chapter 1." Alexander, 116.

7 "The text reverts again to prose to record Jonah's somewhat unconventional, and very unceremonious, return to land." Alexander, 118.

8 "All this time Jonah has been in the fish traveling back to dry land. Now the journey is over. Yahweh speaks to the fish, his instrument of salvation for Jonah. It obediently and doubtless gladly spews up this indigestible object and swims off with a flick of its tail, its distinguished mission accomplished." Allen, 220.

9 "Having experienced in his own life God's power to rescue him from the very jaws of death itself, Jonah, as an expression of his gratitude, promises to offer sacrifices and fulfill his vows to the Lord. His words echo the response of the sailors in 1:16. Finally, Jonah brings his psalm of personal thanksgiving to a climax in the wonderful statement, Salvation comes from the LORD. No other words could summarize better Jonah's appreciation of all that God has done for him. The Lord saves! Ironically, however, it is the very same fact which fills Jonah with intense anger in the final chapter of the book." Alexander, 117-118.

10 "Jonah's time in the fish produced in him a new sense of compassion, consecration, and a new sense of God." Ferguson, 60.

11 "Before we visit Nineveh with him, however, we ought to pause to see the path on which he has come; to marvel at the lengths to which God is prepared to go for his children, and the efforts he is willing to make for them. He will go to any lengths to bring us into the center of his will, no matter what the price may be, either to him or to us. There are few things in the Christian experience more wonderful than this, and few things more awesome." Ferguson, 63.

12 "More perplexing, however, is the fact that Jonah affirms his loyalty to God in a most profound way in the psalm, but then, in the following chapter, he is the reluctant prophet once again. Indeed, in the last chapter he is antagonistic toward God as well. In answer to this issue, it is only necessary to say that Jonah is not a flat, but a complex character. This is, in his spiritual ups and downs he acts like a real person. This roundness of character is one of the reasons that Jonah is such a fascinating and rich book." Longman and Dillard, 447.

DAY 1

Week 6: The Prophet's Proclamation and Penitent Pagans

Jonah 3:1-9

Have you ever lost your temper? That's a funny expression. When I "lose" my temper, I know exactly where it is because it is controlling my body and mood at the time! At my workplace, we have a special display area for employee photography. When three of my shots from a recent trip were accepted by the review board, I thought the hard part was over, but I was so wrong; the difficult part had just begun.

The organizer of the display gave me details of exactly how to prepare my prints, and I spent more than $50 enlarging my photos and buying custom cut mat boards and acid-free mounting glue. I looked forward to walking down the hallway and seeing my photos hung with pride with my name emblazoned below them. However, when I brought my prints in, the organizer took one look at them, curled her lip, and flatly rejected them. She advised me to buy a different kind of mounting tape and informed me that each print had to be double mounted for uniformity.

I was more than a little miffed. I didn't react with harsh words, but with the most insidiously destructive kind of anger—passive aggressiveness. My heart was boiling—and I made sure to make that clear. I felt justified in my anger. After all, I'd spent a ton of money to donate my art. I stormed out of her office.

Two weeks later I was back in her office with my prints, having spent more money on the appropriate changes. She surveyed my adjustments and said my work was still not up to par. I'd like to say that I responded calmly and with grace, but I'm sorry to say I blew it. I again responded with incredulous resentment and heavy sarcasm. Later, after talking with several friends, repeatedly justifying my own anger, I cooled down and realized I had to apologize, which I did. But the damage was already done. I didn't control my temper and I would never be able to take that back.

Even when we get second chances, they aren't always happier endings. I wrote an apology email saying that if I had the chance to do it again, I would react differently. I hope that's true. For the next three months when I would see my prints hanging in the hallway, they only served to remind me of my repeated failures.

It is at times like these that I am thankful that God is merciful and that I cannot exhaust His patience. We don't deserve second chances, but He lovingly works through our failures time and time again for His good purposes.

Express Delivery

1. Chapter 3 begins with a second chance for Jonah. When have you been given a second chance in life? What did you do differently?

2. Read Jonah 3:1-9. Where have you seen the exact same wording as 3:1-3 before?[1]

3. Circle every form of the word "arise" (ESV) in Jonah 3:1-3. What is different about the directional terms in chapter 3 as opposed to chapter 1? Why?[2]

4. How is Nineveh described? How long would it take to journey in Nineveh, according to v. 3? How far was Jonah into Nineveh when he began preaching?[3] Why are these details included, do you think?

5. Record Jonah's proclamation below. Why do you think his message is so brief? Do you think it has to do with his attitude, the author's purpose, or shock value?[4,5] Explain.

6. Imagine you were called to go to a certain foreign superpower and tell its people that God was going to blow them away for their sins in forty days. How would you write that speech? Would you be direct like Jonah, or choose a different tactic?

7. Name at least two other biblical stories in which the span of forty days was integral.[6] What is the significance of this number in these stories?[7]

DAY 2

8. Read Genesis 18:22-19:29. What similarities and differences do you note between the cities/outcomes of Sodom and Gomorrah and Nineveh?

Similarities Between Cities/Outcomes	Differences Between Cities/Outcomes

9. Now compare and contrast Abraham's and Jonah's roles as mediators in the two stories.

Similarities Between Mediators	Differences Between Mediators

Message Received

10. How do the Ninevites react to Jonah's proclamation?

The account of the Ninevites' reaction doesn't make complete sense chronologically. Do you remember the arrangement of Jonah's prayer called synopsis/resumption-expansion? It was like a newspaper report with the main gist of the story up front, followed by more details afterwards. It happens again here with the description of the Ninevites' reaction. Put a box around the synopsis and put a big bracket in the margin as far as the expansion goes.

11. What five actions did the King perform after hearing Jonah's message?[8]

12. What did the King's proclamation require of all Ninevites?[9,10] List the requirements, and then go back through your list and put a heart next to the ones that are internal, not just outward, signs of repentance.

13. What is the King's hope in issuing this proclamation? When he says "Who knows?," it's not a cosmic shrug at fate or our modern expression of desperation. Read Joel 2:12-14 and 2 Sam. 12:22 for other instances of the phrase. What does it mean in these contexts?[11]

14. Why would God have mercy on the Ninevites, a people not "chosen" by Him? How does it change your thinking to know that you serve a "Who knows?" God?

DAY 3

15. Read Psalm 32:1-5 and 1 John 1:8-10. According to these passages, what are the hallmarks of true repentance?

16. Do you think the Ninevites' repentance was sincere? How does the text support your position?

17. We sometimes superficially repent of a sin, when in fact we still harbor secret plans to return to it. What's the difference between superficial repentance and real, heartfelt repentance? How would your best friend be able to tell the difference in you?

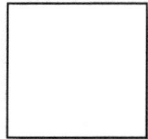

18. What is God is calling you to repent of today? What obstacles are holding you back? What is your first step? Do business with God in this space, then praise the name of the "Who knows?" God who honors repentance with forgiveness and second chances!

[1] "After Jonah's remarkable rescue and restoration to terra firma, he is again instructed to go to Nineveh. This time he makes no attempt to escape from the Lord's presence, but willingly complies. By paralleling here the book's opening remarks, almost word for word, the author skillfully conveys the idea that Jonah is being offered a new beginning. In spite of his earlier refusal, he has a fresh opportunity to fulfill the divine commission." Alexander, 118.

[2] "Jonah is now as compliant as those other servants, the wind, the sea, and the fish." Allen, 221.

[3] "But Jonah had scarcely seen one-third of its streets and market places before God seemed to take hold of him and Nineveh through him, and shake them both to the roots of their beings." Ferguson, 76.

[4] "The prophet's preaching is reluctant and contained in a single verse (3:4), which does not even mention God's name." Longman and Dillard, 443.

[5] "In all likelihood Jonah probably addressed those he encountered at greater length than this. The author, however, playing down Jonah's ability as an orator, condenses his message into five words in Hebrew." Alexander, 120.

[6] A few that came to our minds: Noah's ark (Gen. 7), Moses on the mountain (Exo. 34), Moses' intercession after golden calf (Deut. 9:18, 25), Elijah "on the run" (1 Kings 19), Christ's temptation (Matt. 4, Mark 1, Luke 4), Christ's resurrection to ascension (Acts 1).

[7] "If the forty does its proper work, life begins in a new way. If the forty is ignored, life is destroyed: the ark shipwrecks and everyone is drowned; the Israelites troop back to Egypt to spend the rest of their lives making bricks without straw; Jesus takes up the devil's agenda and the world falls under the rule of antichrist, glad to be rid of the cross; Jesus disappears in the Ascension and the world goes back to business as usual. In Nineveh, the forty did its proper work: the people heard the message not as prediction of doom but as proclamation of hope. Religious Nineveh was doomed, but another way of life was possible, a way of faith in God. Change was possible. They didn't have to live the way they did. They could live for God, before God, in response to God." Peterson, *Under the Unpredictable Plant*, 143-44.

[8] "In these actions of repentance, [the King] symbolizes his human frailty and worthlessness." Alexander, 122.

[9] "As a consequence of trusting God, they declared a fast, and...put on sackcloth. This was a common means in the ancient world of expressing grief, humility and penitence—the hallmarks of true repentance.... The sackcloth used was a thick coarse cloth, normally made from goat's hair; to wear it symbolized the rejection of earthly comforts and pleasures." Alexander, 122.

[10] "It was a Persian custom for animals to participate in mourning ceremonies. Although alien and odd, the gesture would impress forcibly upon the listening circle the sincerity of Nineveh's repentance. The community was threatened with the destruction of all animate life; it was fitting that animals who were to share the fate of their human masters should join in the appeal. The section builds up an impression of the totality of Nineveh's repentance by mentioning the mourning of great and small, king and commoner, man and beast." Allen, 224.

[11] In these passages, "Who knows?" is always associated with a strong hope in God's mercy and His responsiveness to true repentance. Kapur, n.p.

DAY 1

Week 7: The Prophet's Perplexing Response

Jonah 3:10-4:2

If I were the author of a story called Jonah: The Fairytale, I wouldn't have written chapter four. I mean, it doesn't leave us with any warm fuzzies, does it? The end of Jonah leaves the reader hanging, looking for more, with what seems like more questions than answers. Instead, as the author of Jonah: The Fairytale, I would have simply added a concluding verse at the end of chapter three. The book should finish with Jonah 3:11, "And Jonah began his long journey to Israel, rejoicing at the mercy and the goodness of the LORD." I would have titled that section of the Bible study "The Praising Prophet." It would tie a neat little bow on the book as a whole. It would conclude evenly, be balanced, and contain a moral nugget about the importance of obedience. We could imagine ourselves reading Jonah: The Fairytale to our children at bedtime.

But the real shock comes at the moment which should have been Jonah's greatest. Instead of going on his way rejoicing, Jonah erupts in rage at the Lord's mercy toward the Ninevites. The book should have concluded nicely, neatly, optimistically—but it didn't. Jonah preached a small sermon to a great and powerful city. Nineveh was brought literally to its knees in repentance. Yet Jonah could not enjoy it: "Nineveh's positive response to Jonah's preaching so infuriated him that he charged God with evil and asked God to kill him on the spot!"[1] Sometimes after our greatest triumphs we made our biggest mistakes.

The Fruit of Repentance

1. Think of a time when someone (or a group) reacted much more positively than you were expecting him/them to. What was the situation? How did it make you feel?

2. Read Jonah 3:10. What was God's reaction to the Ninevites' change of heart?

3. What does it mean for God to *relent* in 3:10 (KJV *repent*, NIV *have compassion*)?

4. List all characters or persons who have repented and/or had a change of heart up to this point in the book of Jonah.

5. Read Malachi 3:6 and James 1:17. What quality of God do these verses discuss?

6. How is it possible for God to be all-knowing and yet change His mind?[2]

7. What does it mean to you in your current challenges to know that God's character is unchanging and His plan is established, yet that He graciously dialogues with us and is quick to change His disposition towards us when we repent?

DAY 2

Party Pooper

8. Think of a time when someone reacted significantly more negatively than you anticipated. What was the situation? Why was their reaction so much worse than you predicted?

9. Read Jonah 4:1-4. How did Jonah react to God's mercy towards the Ninevites?

10. The Hebrew word *ra'ah* is used three times in 3:10-4:1 to mean "evil, disaster" or "discomfort." The Ninevites turned from their *ra'ah*, God relented of His *ra'ah*, and in 4:1 the author says "it was a great *ra'ah* to Jonah."[3] When you look at these three scenarios, which one of these is "not like the others," and what point is the author making by using the same word?

11. How is Jonah's reaction to God's mercy different here than at the end of chapter 2? Why is it different? Give three possible reasons.

12. What does this tell you about Jonah's heart? His attitude towards outsiders?

13. What does this tell you about God's heart towards outsiders? Jonah's view of God?

☐

14. Read Psalm 145:8-9 and Joel 2:13. How does God describe Himself in these verses?

15. Verse 2 finally reveals Jonah's rationalization for his original disobedience. How does he justify his previous actions? How does this also provide insight into his present attitude toward God's mercy?[4]

16. Now that we can see his heart...is this what you would expect from someone who had the experience of 1:17-2:10? How sincere was Jonah's repentance at the end of chapter 2? Use specific verses to support your view.[5,6]

17. Read Matthew 18:23-35. How does this parable parallel Jonah's story? Which character in the parable most corresponds to Jonah's attitude problem?

18. Jonah knew God's character, and He appreciated the benefits of His attributes in his own life, but he didn't want to share those attributes with just anyone. Do you have enemies that you hope God would "exclude" from His benefits because you feel they are undeserving (even if they repented)?

19. Or, similar to an older sibling's fears about sharing his/her parents with a new baby, do you ever fear that if others gain your "special" relationship with God, it will dilute your own value or importance to God?

20. Read Psalm 139:23-24. Write a prayer thanking God for mercifully taking on the *ra'ah* that you deserve, and ask Him to search your heart and reveal how it needs to become more like His: gracious, compassionate, slow to anger, abounding in love, and quick to forgive and relent.

[1] Keller, 143.

[2] "Neither God's plan nor His will is reversed, nor His volition altered; but what He had from eternity foreseen, approved, and decreed He pursues in uninterrupted tenor, however sudden the variation may appear in men's eyes." John Calvin, *Institutes of the Christian Religion*, Ed. John T. McNeill, 1.17.13 (Philadelphia: Westminster Press, 1960), quoted in Estelle, 120.

[3] Futato, 1690; Kapur, n.p.

[4] "Yahweh now has a rebel on his hands: his agent of salvation, though compelled to do his will, is by no means convinced of its correctness." Allen, 230.

[5] "In the light of his earlier experience it is ironic that Jonah now desires to die on account of God's gracious and compassionate nature. Had he himself not benefited from these very attributes when confronted by death? And had he not rejoiced that *Salvation comes from the Lord*? Clearly, he fails to see the incongruity of his own prayers." Alexander, 127.

[6] "One of Jonah's quintessential problems is that he has forgotten God's mercy toward him. Jonah is suffering from a memory problem. He too has experienced God's mercy, but now he is ill-equipped to appreciate God's mercy when he observes it exercised on someone else's behalf." Estelle, 126.

DAY 1

Week 8: The Parched and Petulant Prophet

Jonah 4:3-11

What do you do when life doesn't meet your expectations? When you've worked diligently and done everything you can to make the situation work out, and it just doesn't, where do you turn? When relationships are frustrating and people hurt and irritate you, how do you deal with it?

One tempting strategy for dealing with messiness and pain is to close off our hearts entirely. We think, *If I don't care or don't love, then I can't be hurt.* This is perhaps the most destructive kind of coping. We can be untouchable in pain, but we will also be numb to joy. We cannot choose just half of that equation. C. S. Lewis in The Four Loves writes: "Love anything and your heart will be wrung and possibly broken. If you want to make sure of keeping it intact you must give it to no one, not even an animal [or a plant, in Jonah's case!]. Wrap it carefully round with hobbies and little luxuries; avoid all entanglements. Lock it up safe in the casket or coffin of your selfishness. But in that casket, safe, dark, motionless, airless, it will change. It will not be broken; it will become unbreakable, impenetrable, irredeemable. To love is to be vulnerable."[1]

I don't want to live hiding my heart from the world, or past hurts, or future uncertainties. I want to live fully right where I am. So what do we do? How do we strike the balance between self-protection and risk? How should we react when trials come?

Several years ago my friend, Erin, was relating to me a conversation she'd had with her mother. "I don't know how to describe what I'm feeling." Erin complained. "It's like I'm covered in wet sand. I keep trying to brush it off my skin, but it irritatingly sticks to me. I can't get rid of it."

"But, Honey," her wise mother replied, "that's how pearls are made. The oyster forms a pearl through the prolonged irritation of a single grain of sand."

To which Erin indignantly exclaimed, "Don't turn my analogy against me, Mom!"

Yet this comparison is inescapably true. We are covered in sand: trials, tribulations, nuisances, and the irritations of life in a sinful world with sinful people. But we should not seek to avoid all such irritants, for they can be used by God to create something beautiful in our lives.

Not a Happy Camper

1. What is irritating you in your life right now? How are you dealing with it?

2. Go through chapter 4 and underline all the words describing emotions. If you want, draw faces in the margin for each one (*Hint:* eyebrows help). What emotion is most frequently mentioned?

3. In your own words, describe why Jonah is angry at God.

4. What is Jonah's wish in verse 3? Why is this surprising, even funny?[2]

5. What is the Lord's question to Jonah in verse 4? What is the emotion behind this question, or what tone of voice do you imagine God used?

6. Can you think of a time when God could have fairly addressed this question to you? What would your reaction have been?

7. Take a look back at pages 13-15 and review the chiasm that covers the book of Jonah. According to the chiasm outline, what section of Jonah contains the focal point—the unique section that deviates from the previous pattern?

8. Is it easier for you to relate to Jonah in chapter one, as a disobedient runaway, or in chapter four, as a pouting judge?[3] Explain.

Jonah and the Beanstalk

DAY 2

9. After Jonah's passionate plea to God, what actions does Jonah take in verse 5? Why?[4]

10. Who appointed the plant (some translations have vine, gourd, ricinus, or leafy tree)? What was its purpose?

11. How does Jonah feel about the plant? How long was the plant in existence?[5]

12. What were the next two items in God's appointment book? How do they make Jonah feel?

13. God's sovereignty over nature is on display again. List all the natural events God sovereignly appoints and superintends in the book up to this point.

14. What is Jonah's reaction to this turn of events? What is God's initial response?

15. Summarize God's final response (v. 10-11) in your own words. [6,7]

16. What does "pity" (NIV concerned about) mean in this context? What do you think the idiom "not know their right hand from their left" means? [8]

17. God is not just the Weatherman with the magic beans. What else is He sovereign over, besides the forces of nature, according to verses 10-11?

DAY 3

18. What is God's purpose in the appointment of the plant, worm, and wind? What does He want Jonah to feel or realize, and why? [9] Let's take a stab at this question by filling in the chart on the next page.

		Plant's Destruction	Ninevites' Salvation
Jonah's Perspective	What is at stake? (What is he most concerned about, either personally or as a representative of Israel?)		
	What is "unfair"? (What makes him mad?)		
	How does God seem to act? (Is He consistent? Justified?)		
God's Perspective	What is at stake? (What is most valuable to Him?)		
	What is unfair? (*Hint*: "Do you do well?")		
	How is God really acting? (Is He consistent? What aspects of His character are shown?)[10]		

19. What in your life seems unfair or a wrong decision on God's part? Are you disproportionally or unjustifiably angry about something? What does the author of Jonah show you about God's perspective?

20. Do you ever feel that God is vicious or vindictive, inconsistent, absentminded, or haphazard? What does the author of Jonah show you about God's perspective?

21. In *Counterfeit Gods*, Tim Keller writes:

   "God confronted Jonah with the fact that he was more upset about his sunburn than he was about thousands of people who 'did not know their right hand from their left.' His idolatrous love for his own country and his moral self-righteousness had removed Jonah's compassion for the great cities and nations of the world. All he cared about was his own country."[11]

   Let that sink in. What are you currently spending your energy and emotions on that is very unimportant in God's eyes? What does the author of Jonah show you about God's perspective?

22. Read Isaiah 55:8-11. With these verses and this perspective in mind, write a prayer committing your thoughts and feelings to the Lord, remembering that He is God and He is using everything in your life to form you into the image of His Son.

[1] C. S. Lewis, The Beloved Works of C.S. Lewis: Surprised By Joy, Reflections on the Psalms, The Four Loves, The Business of Heaven (Grand Rapids: Family Christian Press, 1986, 1958, 1960, 1984), 278-79.

[2] "It is not possible to assess Jonah's position. Geographically he was outside Nineveh; chronologically he was in days of revival; but spiritually he was almost back to square one again. He was certainly defending what he had done before the beginning to dig himself into the spiritual pit of his former disobedience. But so miserable had he become about both his obedience and his disobedience that, rather than see the matter through, Jonah preferred to die. So he prayed for a kind of divine euthanasia." Ferguson, 99.

[3] "When we are being obedient and successful pastors we are in far more danger than when we are being disobedient and runaway pastors. To give us proper warning, the story shows Jonah obedient far more unattractive than Jonah disobedient: in his disobedience he at least had compassion on the sailors in the ship; in his obedience he has only contempt for the citizens of Nineveh." Peterson, Under the Unpredictable Plant, 31.

[4] "Jonah had set himself up as judge. He blurred the distinction between the creature and the Creator. He arrogated to himself the position of arbitrator of life and death from the humble stance of a sinful human creature. He had not acted in accordance with his station in life. He did not really know before whom he stood. A savage torpor had clouded his mind. A caustic sclerosis had covered his heart. Jonah was looking on the situation with unseeing eyes." Estelle, 132.

[5] "The blazing sun beats down on Jonah's poor head, now bereft of the friendly ricinus [plant]. Enervated by sunstroke and exasperated by the loss of his plant, Jonah's recent zest for life shrivels like the ricinus leaves. The shoe Jonah wanted Nineveh to wear was on his foot now, and it pinched." Allen, 233.

[6] "'Let us analyze this anger of yours, Jonah,' comments Yahweh. 'It represents your concern over your beloved ricinus—but what did it really mean to you? Your attachment to it could not be very deep, for it was here one day and gone the next. Your concern was dictated by self-interest, not by a genuine love. You never had for it the devotion of the gardener. If you feel as badly as you do, what would you expect a gardener to feel like, who tended a plant and watched it grow only to see it wither and die, poor thing? And this is how I feel about Nineveh, only much more so. All those people, all those animals—I made them, I have cherished them all these years. Nineveh has cost me no end of effort, and they mean the world to me. Your pain is nothing to mine when I contemplate their destruction." Allen, 233-234.

[7] "The last word, however, rests with the Lord. By contrasting Jonah's attitude to the gourd with his attitude toward the Ninevites, God highlights where the real absurdity lies. Jonah is filled with compassion regarding a mere plant, yet remains hard-hearted towards the entire population of a city. He shows concern for one small item of God's creation, yet fails to care for a large mass of people, who, like Jonah himself, were made in the divine image. The inconsistency rests not with God but with Jonah." Alexander, 130.

[8] "Not knowing their right hand from their left" is an idiom for being morally and spiritually unaware. Futato, 1691.

[9] "Jonah needed the shade; he needed the rest. But God knew that he needed something more. Rest without repentance is never adequate." Ferguson, 107.

[10] If you are stuck on the chart, just do your best! But if you are a leader and you are really stuck on the chart, here are my answers, reading left to right, row by row: comfort/Israel's enemies helped; gave comfort just to take it away/undeserving; changing mind quickly, vicious, vindictive/changing mind quickly, undue mercy; Jonah's heart, lower life form/more important than plants; Jonah's anger/Jonah's anger; planned, object lesson for Jonah (mercy)/consistent, mercifully, compassionate.

[11] Keller, 150.

DAY 1

Week 9: Reflections on a Stormy Passage (Or, There and Back Again)

I have a pretty high tolerance for uncomfortable situations. I work in a hospital and am daily exposed to broken bodies, bodily functions, and patients in less than their peak conditions, to say the least. But even these experiences did not prepare me for the awkward, cross-cultural mess I found myself in one summer.

I had travelled to Hungary twice before so I wasn't really nervous about the food, climate, hosts, or duties. We were staying with Hungarian host families for one week of the mission project. Lindsey, my teammate, and I were introduced to a pleasant, matronly widow named Hijny (pronounced hi-nee) who, though her English was very minimal, appeared overjoyed to host us. While sitting with her at the bus station, our host mom commented on the heat. It was almost unbearable, with record-setting temperatures over 100°F, and no climate control. She fanned herself and said, "We go home and undress." To which Lindsey and I replied, "Yes, we will go to your house and change clothes." Only in hindsight would the foreshadowing be clear.

Hijny didn't mean change clothes. She meant undress.

We weren't in Hijny's house five minutes before she had stripped down totally naked. It seemed that her only weapon against the heat was lack of clothing. Then, free of her apparently oppressive clothing, Hijny began cooking us lunch. She thought nothing of her nudity—cooking, eating lunch, then sitting next to us on the couch to watch TV...all naked.

I have to deal with scantily-clad patients all the time, so it wasn't that I hadn't seen others naked before... but never before had a naked person served me lunch. That was different.

It was uncomfortable, to say the least, to live with Hijny that week. She was naked or wearing minimal clothing most of the time. Her English consisted of a few dozen words. Lindsey and I would arrive after a long bus ride and hike to Hijny's house, exhausted from a day of English camp. We were already spent and not prepared for a night where communication was exhausting, nudity abounded, and cultural faux pas were committed at every turn.

But Jesus called us to love.

It wasn't easy or comfortable as I sat there night after night with my Hungarian dictionary trying to communicate and show love. Trying to find a topic we could discuss without exhausting our vocabulary in the first two sentences. I asked Hijny to teach me Hungarian words and tell me about the pictures around her house. To show me what she enjoyed. What made her who she was. Where her children were.

What her life had been like.

It was exhausting. There's no other way to see it, but it was worth it. I felt totally uncomfortable with a naked 77-year-old grandmother cozied up next to me showing me her photo album. But I did it out of love—love for Jesus and love for Hijny. In spite of the uncomfortableness, the unattractiveness, Christ's work in my heart enabled me to love. And loving, especially when it requires work, is a beautiful thing.

Alternative Endings

1. Look back at week 2 and review your response to questions 13-14 (pages 23-24) about your enemies and opponents. Have any of these relationships changed during the course of the study? Explain.

2. In *What Jesus Demands From the World*, John Piper writes:

   "Jesus' demand that we love our enemies, be merciful, make peace, and forgive assumes that there are people who are hard to love. The demand is expressed in different ways because people are hard to love in different ways. Jesus calls some people our "enemies," which means they are against us. They want to see us fail. Love them, Jesus says (Matt. 5:44; Luke 6:27, 35). Others may not be our personal enemies in this way, but simply people whose character or personality or condition makes them unattractive or even repulsive. Be merciful to them, Jesus says (Matt. 5:7; 18:33; Luke 10:37). Don't base your treatment of them on what they attract or deserve, but on mercy. Others may be our relatives or friends who have taken offense at something we have done—rightly or wrongly—and the relationship is cold or non-existent. Strive to be reconciled to them, Jesus says (Matt. 5:23-26). Others may or may not have anything against you, but you do against them. Forgive them, Jesus says (Matt. 6:14-15). Don't let laziness or pride or anger keep you from the humble work of forgiving, peacemaking, and reconciliation."[1]

Underline the four descriptions of "enemy" that Piper describes above. Circle the four ways Jesus calls us to respond.

Which of these types of "enemy" convicts your spirit today? How do you need to respond?

3. Let's return to the final chapter of the book of Jonah. What does Jonah think he and Israel deserved? What do they really "deserve?"[2]

4. Why do you think the cattle are mentioned in the final verse?

5. Why does the book end so abruptly? What is the author's purpose in this lack of resolution?[3,4]

6. In the spirit of sanctified imagination, write your own "chapter 5" for the book of Jonah.

DAY 2

Internal Inventory

7. If you had to summarize the book of Jonah in a sentence, what would it be?

8. Look back at week one's prayer (page 12) where you laid out your hopes for this study. Were your aspirations met? Explain.

9. What was your favorite part of this study?

10. What aspect(s) of this Bible study had the greatest impact on your life? Why?

11. In what ways can you personally identify with Jonah's story? What character traits (good or bad) do you share with him?[5,6]

12. How does the story of Jonah expand your view of Jesus, the true Jonah?[7,8]

DAY 3

13. Look back at the intro week discussion questions (page 10). How has your understanding of the phrase "Salvation belongs to the LORD" expanded throughout this study?[9,10,11,12]

14. Here is Tim Keller's analysis of Jonah's unresolved ending:

> "The ending is brilliant and satisfying. It's satisfying because we don't need to wonder whether Jonah repented and saw the light. He must have. How do we know? Well, how else would we know the story, unless Jonah told it to someone? And who would ever tell a story in which he is seen as an evil fool on every page, except a man in whom God's grace had reached the center of his heart? Why, though, are we not shown Jonah's response in the book? It is as if God aimed an arrow of loving rebuke at Jonah's heart, set it a-fly, and suddenly Jonah vanishes, leaving us in its path. The question is coming right at us, because you are Jonah and I am Jonah. We are so enslaved to our idols that we don't care about people who are different, who live in the big cities, or who are just in our own families but very hard to love. Are we, like Jonah, willing to change? If we are, then we must look to the Ultimate Jonah, and to his sign, the death and resurrection of Christ."[13]

How is God calling you to respond to His "arrow of loving rebuke"? How do you want your life and heart to be different as a result of this study?

15. Read Psalm 96. Write a prayer thanking Jesus for being the "true Jonah" and asking Him to use you for His glory.

[1] John Piper, *What Jesus Demands From the World* (Wheaton, IL: Crossway, 2006), 212-213.

[2] "It is better to understand Jonah's reluctant and resultant depression as stemming from God's compassion, not just toward a Gentile nation, but a vicious and cruel imperial power that constantly threatened his homeland. Jonah felt Israel deserved better than to have its God forgive its enemies." Longman and Dillard, 448.

[3] "It is primarily the reader on whom God's final words land, the reader who is left to ponder their meaning, the reader who must decide what action to take next." Janet Howe Gaines, *Forgiveness in a Wounded World: Jonah's Dilemma*, Studies in Biblical Literature 5 (Atlanta: Society of Biblical Literature, 1993), quoted in Estelle, 133.

[4] "[The ending] is shaped in a way...to force us to contemplate our personal destiny. It carries no conclusion because it summons us to write the final paragraph. It remains unfinished, in order that we may provide our own conclusion to its message. For you are Jonah; I am Jonah. We recognize ourselves in the story of this man's life. We stand together in need of the mercy of God to enable us, from this day on, to be obedient to his commands, and to live to the praise of his glorious grace." Ferguson, 118.

[5] "The first movement in the story shows Jonah disobedient; the second shows him obedient. Both times Jonah fails. We never do see a successful Jonah. He never gets it right. I find this rather comforting. Jonah is not a model to live up to, a model that shows up my inadequacy; this is training in humility, which turns out to be not a groveling but a quite cheerful humility." Peterson, *Under the Unpredictable Plant*, 11.

[6] "A Jonah lurks in every Christian heart, whimpering his insidious message of smug prejudice, empty traditionalism, and exclusive solidarity. He that has ears to hear, let him hear and allow the saving love of God which has been outpoured in his own heart to remold his thinking and social orientation." Allen, 235.

[7] "When Jesus Christ came to earth, he was leaving the ultimate comfort zone, in order to come and minister not just to a people who *might* harm him, but to people who would. And to save them, he would have to do much more than preach, he would have to die for them. While the original Jonah was merely thought to be dead, Jesus actually died and rose again. It was what Jesus called the sign of Jonah (Matt. 12:31). Consider another way in which Jesus was the ultimate Jonah. In Mark 4 we have an account from Jesus's life that deliberately evoked the Old Testament story. There was a terrible storm and, like Jonah, Jesus was asleep in the midst of it. Like the sailors, Jesus's disciples were terrified and woke him up to say that they were going to perish. In both cases the storm was miraculously calmed and those in the boat were saved by the power of God." Keller, 151.

[8] "Jesus himself compared and contrasted his ministry with the ministry of Jonah. ...He is 'greater than Jonah,' however, because while Jonah reluctantly preached to save a city against his will, Jesus freely gave up his life to save many." Longman and Dillard, 448.

[9] "In the fullness of time, God has in Jesus Christ brought salvation to the nations, not just Israel. The compassion of God revealed so powerfully at the end of Jonah is quintessentially manifested on the hill of Golgotha. All of this foreshadowing in Jonah comes into sharper focus in what God has done in and through Jesus Christ for his own sheep. Truly, "Salvation comes from the Lord" (2:9)." Estelle, 135.

[10] *Salvation comes from the Lord.* It is not the exclusive possession of anyone group, nor does it guarantee their continued existence at the expense of others. To those who appeal, on the basis of their special relationship with God for the overthrow of their enemies, the book of Jonah voices a stern rebuke. God's mercy may extend to the most unlikely of people, and who can tell what the consequences may be?" Alexander, 47.

[11] "The life experience of Jonah prophetically anticipates the day in which restoration will mean the worldwide expansion of God's saving activity among all the nations of the world (see Matt. 12:40). Having experienced exile from the Father in his death, Jesus rises in restoration to commission his disciples that they go and make disciples of all the nations (Matt. 18:18-20)." Robertson, 161.

[12] "The book of Jonah focuses in two ways on God's compassion for those outside of Israel. In the first place, the book contrasts spiritually sensitive pagans with the reluctant Israelite prophet...In the second place, the book ends on a note that focuses on God's feelings toward Nineveh as he rhetorically asks Jonah, 'Should I not have concern for the great city Nineveh?'" Longman and Dillard, 447.

[13] Keller, 153.

Week 10: Binding it to our Hearts

No homework this week! Use this opportunity to go back and finish any questions you had to skip before, and make sure you have drawn a theme icon in each of the theme question boxes.

Directions for Leaders:

1. Be prepared to break your participants up into small groups and randomly assign one icon/theme to each group.

2. If desired, obtain materials for the creative closing activity in advance.

In Small Groups: (20 minutes)

For your group's icon/theme:

1. Skim back through your homework and re-read every question that is marked with your assigned icon (ignore all the other questions!). Think about the following:

2. What is the point, or what did you learn, about that theme from that question?

3. Turn to the appropriate theme page following this page and list all your awesome insights there!

In Large Group: (30 minutes)

For each icon/theme:

1. Share and discuss the small groups' insights. Add to your list as you hear new ideas. Individuals outside the small group theme can contribute as well.

2. As a large group, choose your top three insights for each icon and write a star next to them.

3. Repeat for all the themes, taking notes on the themes you didn't already work on, and choosing your top three insights to star.

4. Close in prayer, asking God to seal this study's insights in our hearts and make these themes real in our lives.

God's Sovereignty

Obedience and Repentance from the Heart

God's Love for the Nations

Afterword: Farewell to the Prodigal, Poetic, Penitent, Petulant Prophet

Jonah is finally done.

Nine months in the writing, this is the closest thing I've experienced to compare with bearing a child. I've experienced months of preparation, sleepless nights, food cravings, and pain as I prepared to "birth" this study. Okay—so maybe the food cravings are unrelated, but still, it's been a long time coming. Like a proud parent, I'm ready to share my little bundle of joy with others.

Writing is both easier and harder than I ever expected. I often feel like Jeremiah when he said, "There is in my heart as it were a burning fire shut up in my bones, and I am weary with holding it in, and I cannot" (Jeremiah 20:9b). I have words, ideas, and thoughts bursting out of me—so I write. Writing for me is both a form of therapy and of art. It helps me to process and give definition to ideas floating around in my heart, and it allows me to paint pictures with keystrokes to be shared with others.

In other ways writing is wearisome because it not only seems to consume all my spare time, but it puts my heart on display in a way nothing else can. You've read some of my stories—not all of them are shining moments, and it takes courage to display my flaws in order to elevate the beauty of God's grace. I also have a totally new respect for the editing process. I think, when I tell people I'm editing a Bible study, more often than not they think I just run spellcheck and am done with it. They don't realize that it involves taking apart the entire study, putting it in a blender set to frappé and then piecing it back together word by word. Editing is painful. I could not have made it through the grueling months of editing without the constant support, prayer, and love of my Editor/Cheerleader extraordinaire, Abby Gjertsen. Writing (and editing!) Bible studies is truly a labor of love.

But now we get to enjoy it! I love hearing other people's observations, opinions, and insights as we discuss and work through the material together. It doesn't matter how long I've studied and how many commentaries I've read, there's always more to be gleaned from Scripture. So thank you for being so encouraging, for sharing your hearts, and for taking this journey with me.

I'm happy to be finished with Jonah. To hold the tangible evidence of all my work is a beautiful thing. But at the same time I'll miss it. I'll miss my weekly three-hour long Skype conversations with Abby to perfect the study. I'll miss sitting cross-legged underneath my coffee table surrounded by dozens of commentaries. I'll miss writing introductions for each week and putting on display the best (and the worst!) of me. I'll miss spending gobs of time with Jonah; he has become a friend of mine.

But the good news is that the study doesn't have to end here. Before you start hyperventilating that there's another week of homework hiding somewhere behind the bibliography page, what I mean is that it's now our responsibility to take what God has taught us about ourselves, each other, and the world through the book of Jonah and put it into practice.

How will you find ways to celebrate God's sovereignty? How will you live a life characterized by love, repentance, and obedience with a pure heart and right motives? How will you align your heart with God's heart to spread the good news to all nations? These are the take-aways from this study. Like I said at the beginning, I don't much care if you can diagram a beautiful chiasm of the book of Jonah if it doesn't change your heart.

So, Beloved, let Jonah's story change you. Be different because of your time spent in a little book, written hundreds of years ago, about a bumbling, pouting prophet and his merciful, compassionate God.

Rejoicing that Salvation Belongs to the LORD,

Kelly

Leaders' Guide

Intro
Week

Intro Week Materials: Each participant will need a copy of Jonah in the English Standard Version (can be printed from biblegateway.com or esv.literalword.com) and a few colored pencils for the first meeting. In addition, have one copy of Jonah from Eugene Peterson's *The Message* (also at biblegateway.com) available to read aloud.

Arrival/Snack time (15 min.)

In Large Group: (up to 35 min.)

1. Begin with a brief get-to-know you activity that helps people learn each other's names. (Consider one of these ideas: Share your name and what kind of footwear you are most like and why; share your name and a theme song for your week so far; share your name and what superpower you wish you had and why; etc.)

2. Ask: Why are you here, or what are you hoping to get out of this study?

3. Open in prayer, thanking God for this opportunity to study His Word and asking the Holy Spirit to fill our needs through it.

4. Read Jonah from *The Message* with your group. You can have each person read a few verses or ask four people to read a chapter each.

Individually: (15 min.)

Hand out the ESV copies of Jonah and colored pencils. Guide participants to read and mark their copies, underlining repeated words and phrases and marking whatever catches their attention and/or seems significant. You can do the first few verses together to get them started, but then set them loose to try it alone!

In Small Groups: (20 min.)

Divide into small groups of 3-5 people and discuss the questions listed in the participant guide.

Back to the Large Group: (15 min.)

Allow small groups to share some of their insights. Try to balance the amount of time groups have to speak. Read the section on themes together aloud or individually.

Close with a prayer asking God's help to be joyfully obedient to complete our homework, and ask Him to bless our sandals off through this study!

Weeks 1-9 Materials: Each participant will need a copy of Jonah in the English Standard Version which they can mark on, something to write with, and his/her participant guide. You might also want to have colored pencils and blank prayer request cards. Most importantly, pray for your study members to have time and the desire to complete their homework, to come and discuss the material, and to be transformed by God's Word.

Weeks 1-9

Preparation: Coordinating Small Groups

Pray for wisdom to know which of your participants would be consistent, caring small group leaders/facilitators (SGLs). Contact potential SGLs and ask if they are willing to facilitate and pray for a small group of participants. Make a list of participants from the Intro Week and prayerfully divide them into permanent small groups with consistent SGLs. Once you have your SGLs confirmed, inform them of their group members so they can begin to pray for them specifically.

Arrival/Snack time (15 min.)

In Large Group: (5-10 min.)

1. For Week 1 (the second meeting), you might want another brief get-to-know you activity that helps people learn each other's names and makes everyone feel welcome. You won't need to do this every subsequent week.

2. Open in prayer, asking for mental focus and teachable hearts, and inviting the Holy Spirit to transform us through His Word.

3. Announce the small group leaders and their assigned members, and tell everyone these will be consistent through the rest of the study.

Small Group Discussion (up to 45 min.)

4. Each week, ask: "Who completed their homework this week?" Offer verbal encouragement for prioritizing that time in the Word, and maybe also stickers, candy, etc., but don't dwell on this long. Encourage everyone to feel free to share during the meeting, whether s/he was able to complete the homework or not.

5. Each week, ask: "What is God teaching you from the study this week?" or, "What had the biggest impact on you this week from our study?" Model sharing yourself, as well as good listening. Let there be some silence if people need that space to think or organize their response. Gently draw out all participants and make sure no one person dominates this time. Encourage participants to support their responses with Scripture where possible.

6. At some point in the discussion, make sure you talk about some part of each day's homework and each of the theme questions (with the boxes for icons). The discussion does not have to go in the order of the questions. Small Group Discussion (up to 40 min.)

Small Group Prayer/Closing (15 min.)

7. Share prayer requests/updates and pray for one another. This can be done in pairs if time is short. Encourage participants to complete next week's homework and attend the next study meeting.

Note: Leaders, please look at the materials needed for Week 10 in advance so you have time to order or shop for the items in the optional closing activity.

Week 10

No homework for Week 10! Use this opportunity to go back and finish any questions you had to skip before, and make sure you have drawn a theme icon in each of the theme question boxes.

Materials needed for optional closing activity:

· three metal charms per person: a heart, a globe, and a crown.[1]

· yarn or embroidery floss in red, blue, and purple

· scissors

· *optional: gold yarn or floss, beads, jewelry clasps, keychain rings, etc.*

Preparation: Small Groups

For this week's activity you will need three or more small groups. If you only have two, you will need to divide them differently just for this week.

Arrival/Snack time (15 min.)

In Large Group: (5-10 min.)

Open in prayer, thanking God for His faithfulness.

Announce that this week we will be going back through the study and focusing on what we learned in each of the theme questions (with the icon boxes next to them). Each small group will be assigned one theme to focus on and review. Group members should re-read all their theme questions and responses with this in mind: "What is the point, or what did you learn, about this theme from this question?" They should discuss and record their answers on the blank theme page that matches their assigned theme (help them find these pages).

We will return to large group in 20 minutes to share our insights.

Divide your people into at least 3 small groups (if possible, keep your regular small groups). If you are doing the optional closing activity: Ask one member of each small group to come up and draw a charm out of a bag to randomly determine which theme they will be focusing on. If you are not doing the closing activity, just randomly assign themes to groups.

In Small Groups: (20 min.)

For your group's assigned theme:

Skim back through your homework and re-read every question that is marked with your assigned theme's icon (ignore all the other questions!). Think about the following:

- What is the point, or what did you learn, about that theme from that question?

- Turn to the appropriate blank theme page and list all your awesome insights there!

- Choose your best three insights and write a star next to them. These will be what you share with the large group!

In Large Group: (20 min.)

- Say: "The purpose of this time is to get everyone's theme pages filled with insights from Jonah! Take notes as you listen to the small groups share, and feel free to share your own insights even if you are not assigned to that theme."

- For each theme: Invite each small group to share the three insights that they starred. Other groups with the same theme can then add any additional insights.

- Close in prayer, asking God to seal this study's insights in our hearts and make these themes real in our lives.

Optional Closing Activity: Charm Bookmarks or Bracelets (25 min.)

Congrats! You've made it to the end of *Jonah: Salvation Belongs to the LORD!* We want you to have a keepsake, something tangible to take away from the study that could serve to remind you of the insights you saw and truths you gained through this study. One way to remember what you've learned is to make a braided Bible bookmark, bracelet, keychain lanyard, or rear view mirror decoration—whatever you will see and/or use—with charms to represent each of our themes in Jonah.

Each person should take some of each color of string, braid them, and tie on the charms in some creative way to make your memory item. Use your imagination and have fun!

The braided pattern is designed to remind you of the three themes interwoven repeatedly and purposefully throughout the book. The three icon charms and the colors of the thread were chosen to represent the themes specifically: a heart (red), a globe (blue), and a crown (purple or gold). My prayer is that this project will be a stone of remembrance (Joshua 4:8-9) in your life that will serve to remind you of what you learned over the course of this study. Happy creating!

---

[1] The heart and crown charms can be easily found at Hobby Lobby, JoAnn's or Michael's; the globes were the hardest to find. I bought them from chubbychicocharms.com.

Bibliography

Alexander, T. Desmond. *Jonah: An Introduction and Commentary*. Downers Grove, IL: IV Press, 1988.

Allen, Leslie C. *The Books of Joel, Obadiah, Jonah and Micah*. New International Commentary on the Old Testament. Downers Grove, IL: William B. Eerdmans, 1976.

Arnold, Bill T. & Bryan E. Beyer. *Encountering the Old Testament*. Grand Rapids: Baker Books, 2008.

Barker, Kenneth L., ed. *The NIV Study Bible*. Grand Rapids: Zondervan, 2002.

Calvin, John. *Institutes of the Christian Religion*. Ed. John T. McNeill. 1.17.13. Philadelphia: Westminster Press, 1960. Quoted in Estelle.

"Cessationists View." *Monergism.com*. CPR Foundation. http://www.monergism.com/directory/link_category/Spiritual-Gifts/Cessationists-View-Articles/.

Elwell, Walter A. "God, Names of." *Baker's Evangelical Dictionary of Biblical Theology* (1996): 1897. https://www.studylight.org/dictionaries/bed/g/god-names-of.html.

Estelle, Bryan D. *Salvation Through Judgment and Mercy: The Gospel According to Jonah*. Phillipsburg, NJ: P&R, 2005.

Ferguson, Sinclair B. *Man Overboard!: A Study of the Life of Jonah*. Wheaton, IL: Tyndale House, 1982.

Futato, Mark. **Jonah. Study Notes in the ESV Study Bible**. Wheaton, IL: Crossway Bibles, 2008.

Gaines, Janet Howe. *Forgiveness in a Wounded World: Jonah's Dilemma*. Studies in Biblical Literature 5. Atlanta: Society of Biblical Literature, 1993. Quoted in Estelle.

Kapur, Eric. "The Book of Jonah." Unpublished class notes, Orlando Grace Church, 2005.

Keller, Timothy. *Counterfeit Gods: The Empty Promises of Money, Sex, and Power, and Only Hope that Matters*. New York: Penguin, 2009.

Lewis, C.S. *The Beloved Works of C.S. Lewis: Surprised By Joy, Reflections on the Psalms, The Four Loves, The Business of Heaven*. Grand Rapids: Family Christian Press, 1986, 1958, 1960, 1984.

Longman, Tremper III and Raymond B. Dillard. *An Introduction to the Old Testament, 2nd ed*. Grand Rapids: Zondervan, 2006.

MacDonald, William. *The Believer's Bible Commentary*. Atlanta: Thomas Nelson Publishers, 1995.

Peterson, Eugene H. *The Message*. Colorado Springs: NavPress, 2002.

---. *Under the Unpredictable Plant: An Exploration in Vocational Holiness*. Grand Rapids: William B. Eerdmans, 1992.

Piper, John. *What Jesus Demands From the World*. Wheaton, IL: Crossway Books, 2006.

"The Refiner's Fire." *The Friend: A Religious and Literary Journal* 77, no. 45 (1904): 357. http://books.google.com/.

Robertson, O. Palmer. *The Christ of the Prophets, Abridged Edition*. Phillipsburg, NJ: P&R, 2008.

Ryken, Leland, James C. Wilhoit, and Tremper Longman III, eds. *Dictionary of Biblical Imagery*. Downers Grove, IL: IV Press, 1998.

Waltke, Bruce K. *An Old Testament Theology*. Grand Rapids: Zondervan, 2007.

Walton, John H. and Andrew E. Hill. *Old Testament Today*. Grand Rapids: Zondervan, 2004.